How You Can Sell Options For a Living

A Practical Guide on How to Extract Income from the Markets

SHMULIK KARPF

Copyright © 2013 Shmulik Karpf
All rights reserved.
ISBN: 1492976806
ISBN 13: 9781492976806
Library of Congress Control Number: 2013920898
CreateSpace Independent Publishing Platform
North Charleston, South Carolina

**To my wonderful wife, Ayala,
and our magnificent Emily**

*"For I don't care too much for money,
for money can't buy me love."*

—The Beatles

Table of Contents

Introduction · vii
Chapter 1: The "Secret" World of Options · · · · · · · · · · · 1
Chapter 2: The Language of Options · · · · · · · · · · · · · · · 5
Chapter 3: Why Sell Options? · · · · · · · · · · · · · · · · · · · 15
Chapter 4: My Strategy—General Guidelines · · · · · · · · 21
Chapter 5: My Seven-Step Strategy—Step by Step · · · · · 33
Chapter 6: Your Obligation Is Due · · · · · · · · · · · · · · · 55
Chapter 7: How to Turn a Losing Trade into a Winner · 61
Chapter 8: How to Place and How to Close a Trade · · · 65
Chapter 9: The Alpha of Technical Analysis · · · · · · · · 71
Chapter 10: A Real Trade from Start to Finish · · · · · · · 79
Chapter 11: Options and Trading Psychology · · · · · · · 85
Chapter 12: Four Very Important Don'ts · · · · · · · · · · · 93
Chapter 13: Trading and You · · · · · · · · · · · · · · · · · · · 99
Appendix · 103
About the Author · 107

Introduction

It's now 2013, and it has been five long years since interest rates were first slashed to 0 percent. These are tough times for savers and retirees who counted on their money growing at the average 4–5 percent rate they were used to. What's worse is that it seems like the end of this 0 percent era is far from over. Today, perhaps more than in any other time in history, people must come up with creative ways to make extra income every month.

In this book, I will describe and explain in detail my seven-step strategy that I've been using for the past ten years to extract a monthly paycheck from the market. I believe this trading strategy is one of the safest trading strategies that you can possibly find. And even more importantly—it's relatively simple to implement.

Believe me, I have tried pretty much each and every trading strategy known to mankind. This strategy is the most lucrative strategy with the most minimal risk out there.

My strategy doesn't require a BA in physics or a PhD in finance. In fact, most physicists and economic wizards will probably fail to see a dime from implementing this strategy. You, on the other hand, can earn a consistent and reliable stream of income from it.

But before we even get started, it's essential that I tell you what you *should not* expect from this book. This book isn't a quick "how to get rich in one year" guide, nor is it a "how to make 50 percent a year on your money in the stock market" manual. If you're looking for such a manual, kindly close this book and proceed down the aisle. I'm sure you'll find many such guides with tempting headlines there. The trouble with these books is that the most successful item in the book isn't the content but the headline. These types of quick guides usually lead to financial ruin for everyone but their highly motivated authors.

Now that we have discussed what you *should not* expect from this book, I can tell you what you *can and should* expect from it. At the end of this book, you will learn how to successfully implement a trading strategy that has returned me between 15 percent and 22 percent a year, each and every year, for the past ten years.

I will walk you through the nuts and bolts of my seven-step strategy. I will explain why this is even possible in a rational financial market. And why this opportunity is something that will exist for many, many more years to come. There's absolutely no reason why you shouldn't take advantage of my strategy and earn a consistent monthly income for yourself.

Now, if you've decided that you wish to give it a try, I'm more than glad to welcome you aboard. I urge you to pick up my book and begin to learn my steady, consistent way to riches.

Chapter 1:
The "Secret" World
of Options

Over the years, I have come to realize that options are probably the most misunderstood segment of the financial world. Take a moment and think about it. I am sure that at some point in time, you probably bought a few shares or bonds here and there, but I'm pretty confident that you have never engaged in the sale or purchase of options. It's just not that common for the retail investor/trader. It's a field dominated by professional investment powerhouses.

This has caused a lot of confusion and ignorance surrounding the field of options selling. One of the goals of this book is to demystify the field of options and teach you how you can make a consistent living from it.

But before you do that, you must first understand that anything in the financial markets is a battle of interests. The only reason you haven't been taught a thing about options is that the heavyweight professionals don't want you to be. By leaving amateur investors out of the game, they get the chance to make hundreds of thousands of dollars each and every month from selling options. The last thing these traders wish to do is to let you join the party. They would much rather have you on the opposite side of their trade.

And it isn't only the investment houses that are hiding this income-generation secret from you. Your broker and financial advisor are on this boat too. There are three main reasons why brokers and investment advisors don't want you to learn how to earn a monthly income by selling options.

One reason is that options require less capital for investment. Because you need to invest fewer dollars when you buy options (we'll talk about leverage in the next chapter), brokers make less money from commissions and trading fees. The last thing a broker wishes to do is to teach you a trading strategy that will bring in fewer and fewer commissions per month. You can't blame him for that. He'll be cutting the branch on which he sits.

Another reason why your broker will never tell you about options is that, well, it's simply a headache for him. There's really no reason why your broker would take upon himself such a burden to educate you about options and how to make money on them. The more you call him and the more time of his you consume, the less time he has to recruit new clients. In a sense, you would be eroding his profit margins.

The third reason why your broker won't discuss options with you is that he probably doesn't know how to earn a consistent stream of income from options. Don't forget that your broker isn't some supertrader for Goldman Sachs. Many brokers are simply not informed enough to be able to consistently beat the market at its own game. If they were, they probably wouldn't work as brokers but as traders.

But have no worries. At the end of this book, the world of options will cease to be a mystery to you, and instead it will become a reliable source of income. So let's begin our journey.

Chapter 2:
The Language of Options

Before you begin to learn how to sell options for a living, you must first speak the language of options. This chapter will give you all the basics you need to know on options. As always, I won't burden you with unnecessary information. You'll get only the important material that's relevant for your trading. We'll leave anything else to the academia. So let's get started.

What's an option?

An option is the right to buy or sell an asset at a certain price and by a certain date. So, for example, you can purchase an option today that gives you the right to buy shares of IBM at $150 in February 2014. Our very first step in learning my strategy is to understand the special traits that options have—and other financial instruments, like stocks, don't. There are three main traits that distinguish options from other financial instruments like bonds or stocks.

Trait #1: An option is a derivative.

An option, by its very nature, is a derivative. This means that the price of an option isn't a stand-alone, rather it is *derived* from the price of another underlying asset. This way, equity options derive their price from the price of the equity (stocks), and bond options derive their price from the price of bonds. For example, options on the giant software company Microsoft derive their price directly from the price of Microsoft's shares. So the quoted price of the stock has a major impact on the price of the option. My strategy only deals with equity options, so we're not really interested in any other type of options.

Trait #2: All options expire.

Every option has a limited life span. In contrast to stocks and similar to milk, all options have an expiration date. They do not last forever. At the end of their specified time period, options are either converted into stocks (we'll talk about that later), or simply delisted from trade. Say, for example, that we're now in August 2013. You can decide to buy options that expire in September, October,

November, and so on. You can even buy options that expire as long as two years down the road. For technical reasons, the expiration date is always the third Friday of each month. Once an option expires, it's worth zero dollars—nil, nothing.

Trait #3: Options and leverage

Options involve leverage. You must understand the notion of leverage that's embedded in options. Each option represents one hundred shares.[1] This means that you can either buy one hundred shares of your favorite stock in the open market or simply purchase one option contract for only a fraction of the cost. For example, a hundred shares of Microsoft (currently trading at $32) will cost you $3,200 (one hundred times $32). If, on the other hand, you choose the path of options, you can buy a single call option on Microsoft for only $320 and obtain the same market exposure to Microsoft.

A Call Option

A call option gives its buyer the right (but *not* the obligation) to buy shares at a predetermined price at a certain

---

[1]   Recently, minioptions have been introduced. Each "mini" option controls only ten shares, not one hundred.

point in time in the future. The price of such a right is called a premium. This is what the buyer of this call option will pay to obtain the right to buy the stock for the predetermined price sometime in the future. Let's use the example below to make sure we're on the same track here.

On September 10, 2013, shares of beverage giant Coca-Cola (KO) changed hands for roughly $38. You can sell a *call option*, which expires on November 19, 2013 with a strike price of $38. For this option you sell, the buyer will pay you $117. That's the premium, or the price, of that option. This means that you sold someone the right (but *not* the obligation) to buy shares of Coke from you in November at a price of $38 a share. For this future right, he paid you $117 today.

So basically, the buyers of call options are folks who are optimistic about the company. They are bullish, and they believe that the share price will trend higher from here.

A Put Option

A put option gives its buyer the right (but *not* the obligation) to sell shares at a predetermined price at a certain point in time in the future. The price of such right is called a premium. This is what the buyer of this put option will pay to obtain the right to *sell* the stock for the predetermined price sometime in the future. Let's use the same example as above...

On September 10, 2013, shares of Coca-Cola changed hands for roughly $38. You can sell a *put option*, which expires on November 19, 2013 with a strike price of $38. For this option you sell, the buyer will pay you $100. That's the premium, or the price, of that option. This means that you sold someone the right (but *not* the obligation) to sell you shares of Coke in November at a price of $38 a share. For this future right, that someone paid you $100 today.

In contrast to folks who buy call options, put buyers are obviously pessimistic about the stock. They are betting on a decline in the price of shares.

A Strike Price

Options come in a large variety of strike prices. A strike price is simply the price reference for a given stock. So you've got many strike prices to choose from. Say Coca-Cola is now selling for $40, and you strongly believe that shares could easily climb to $42. What you will do is buy a call option on Coca-Cola *at the $42 strike*. You can do the same with the $44 strike, the $45 strike, or any other strike price that you can possibly think of.

Time frame

One of the inherent traits of any option is that it has a limited life span. At the end of which, it expires and is delisted from trade. Just as there are numerous strike prices to choose from, there are numerous time frames for any option.

Suppose, for example, that now is August 2013. You can go ahead and buy an option that expires in one month (September 2013 expiration), in two months (October 2013 expiration) or even 10 months from now (June 2014 expiration).

A time frame of less than 3 months to expiration is regarded as a short- term option, and a time frame of longer than 10 months is regarded as a long- term option.

My strategy focuses on options with 3- 4 months to expiration. I will explain why later on.

Volatility

Volatility is simply the extent of movement that the security experiences relative to the market. A stock that goes up 5 percent a day and then drops 5 percent another day is much more volatile than a stock that rises by 0.2 percent one day and drops 0.2 percent another day.

Why should we care about volatility?

We care a lot about volatility because high volatility makes option premiums (prices) go up. This means that as volatility ticks up, we—as option sellers—gain more from the sale of every option. It's as simple as that.

Out of the Money (OTM) Options

Out of the money (OTM) refers to options that have no "real" value in them. I'm intentionally oversimplifying this, but I'll elaborate on this topic later on in this book. Specifically, a call option is OTM if its strike price is currently higher than the market price of the underlying asset. A put option is OTM if its strike price is currently lower than the market price of the underlying asset.

For example, if shares of Coke are now trading for $40 a share, a call option at the $45 strike price is OTM. It's considered "out of the money" because shares must climb by $5 just so the option is at break-even point.

The same applies for a put option. If shares of Coke are now trading for $40 a share, a put option at the $38 strike price is OTM. It's considered "out of the money" because shares must decline by an extra $2 just so the option is at break-even point.

The flip side to OTM options is the ITM (in the money) options. Specifically, a call option is ITM if its strike price is currently lower than the market price of the underlying asset. A put option is ITM if its strike price is currently higher than the market price of the underlying asset. Remember, "in the money" means the options have real value if they were exercised today.

The cousin of OTM options and ITM options is ATM options (at the money). A call option or a put option is ATM if its strike price is currently at the market price of the underlying asset. This way, a $42 call (or put) option on Coke is ATM as long as shares of Coke are trading for $42.

The reason we care so much whether an options is OTM, ITM, or ATM is simple. My strategy encourages you to sell OTM and ATM options, and refrain from selling ITM options. That's because ITM options have real value in them, and that's why they involve a higher degree of risk for us as option sellers. I will always prefer to sell options that have no real intrinsic value. This type of options will lose its value much more quickly than ITM options.

Putting It All Together

Once you digest all the information above, you'll see that each and every option has its own unique ID. There aren't two options with the same ID. For example, a call option to buy shares of Coca-Cola in November 2013, for a price of $42, will look like this: **KO November 2013 $42 Call**.

Let's dissect the option's ID. The first most important component of the ID is the stock's ticker. In this case, we want to buy options on Coca-Cola, whose ticker is *KO*. The option's ID always begins with the symbol of the underlying asset.

The next component of the ID is the expiration date of the option, expressed in terms of a month and year. In our case, this option expires in November 2013. It's as simple as that.

The third component is the strike price. In this specific ID, the trader bought the $42 strike price. This means that if shares of Coke are currently trading for $40, this option is out of the money by $2. That's because the strike price is two dollars higher than the prevailing market price for shares of Coke. If, for example, the trader bought options at the $40 strike, all being equal—his options would be at the money. Again, that's because the strike price is equal to the market price of the shares at the time.

The fourth and last component of the ID is the direction you're betting on. If you want to go long (bullish) such as this case—a call option is what you need—and vice versa—if you're pessimistic about a stock, a put option is the right way to go.

I know you thought that options were a mystery and that it took years and tons of written material to master them. The fact is that in these very few pages of information lies all the basic information that you need in order to successfully sell options for a living. This information is mandatory. Anything beyond it is simply not necessary.

If the field of options is absolutely new to you, I encourage you to read chapter 2 again. It will help you digest the new terminology of options. After you're ready, you can proceed to chapter 3, which explains why you can and should sell options.

Chapter 3:
Why Sell Options?

Before I begin to describe and explain my simple, seven-step trading strategy, it's important to devote a chapter to the unique traits of my option-selling strategy. After all, there are so many trading strategies out there!

This chapter will describe four great advantages of option selling and why my strategy is so different from so many trading strategies out there. So let's begin.

Advantage #1: Exit Worry-Free

Before any trade is placed, a trader must first visualize to himself very clearly how he or she intends to exit from the trade. In other words, every good trade must begin with a well-thought-out exit plan. The tricky part is that it's extremely difficult to pinpoint the optimal exit price. With markets being what they are, prices swing sharply to reflect the hottest news—and the exit plan quickly becomes irrelevant.

And you might think to yourself that exiting from a trade isn't such a great problem as long as the trade is profitable. But that isn't the case. Thousands of books have been written on how to calculate (and stick to) your own exit plan. It appears that exiting from a trade is one of the most complicated and frustrating tasks that a trader faces.

My option-selling strategy saves you all the hassle. There's no need to plan and worry about an exit strategy, because the exit point is already embedded in the trade. You see, when we sell options, these very options come with a specific expiration date. This means that after this date— no matter what happens—the trade is done and complete. So, for example, if we sold a September put option on Intel in the month of June, in three months this option won't exist. They are delisted from trade in September. Whenever we sell an option, it's always with a predetermined time-frame stamp on it. After that time period expires, we're out of the trade.

Therefore, selling options, by definition, unburdens us from the conventional worry of all traders—the worry of when to get out.

Advantage #2: Action-Free

Almost all trading strategies are highly action oriented. They require constant action on your part. Trust me on this—I have tried almost every trading strategy out there. In almost all cases, the trading strategy requires that you sit in front of your PC for at least a couple of hours each day staring at graphs and charts while trading session takes place. Otherwise, you'll lose money. That's because almost all trading strategies out there aim to take advantage of small mispricing in stocks here and there. You must be alert and ready at all times, or you simply won't make money.

In contrast to common trading strategies, my option-selling strategy requires almost no action on your part after the trade has been placed. You're free to go fishing, read a good book, or ride your bicycle around town. In fact, the less you do, the better. In a sense, my strategy encourages inactivity.

That's not to say that selling options requires no time. I would be deceiving you if I made such a statement. Option selling requires your full time and attention. But it requires it only *before* a trade is made. After you have placed the trade, there's nothing for you to actually do but wait until expiration day arrives.

Selling options is similar to writing insurance policies. A sensible insurance company certainly devotes time and thought prior to writing a policy. But it doesn't spend each and every day monitoring the current state of its policies. It only reviews policies right before they expire.

Therefore, my option-selling strategy will make you money *and* free up your time. This advantage shouldn't be taken lightly.

Advantage #3: Capital-Free (Almost)

Most trading strategies are capital intensive. By that I mean that the trader is required to allocate most (if not all) of his funds to his trading brokerage account. The fewer dollars he commits, the less money he or she is bound to make.

But this isn't the case with my option-selling strategy. When you sell (write) options, you're not required by your broker to put down the total amount of funds. That's because the sale of options creates the *possible* future obligation to buy in shares. The key word here is "possible." Since the occurrence of such an event is far from certain, you're allowed not to invest anything today.

You see, with my strategy you get to make a monthly income *and* leave most of your capital in your account.

The only thing that your broker must demand is that you place 20 percent of the trade's worth in cash dollars in your account. That's simply to make sure you don't run away with your obligation to some distant place on the globe. But other than that 20 percent margin requirement, you're not obligated to put down any capital. And even that 20 percent is sitting in your own account earning interest.

Not having to a lot of capital is a great advantage, because it substantially increases your ROI (return on investment), and it enables you to earn a great return on the capital that you did commit. You can invest the rest of the money in other profitable opportunities.

Advantage #4: Time-Free

I have never met a person who was able to stop time. Time is always on the move, and that's why selling options is such a great idea. You see, when you sell an option, part of the price you receive is for the time that's left in the option. So, for example, if you sell an option that's three months away from expiration day, you will be paid for three months' worth of time.

With every day that passes, the option (that you just sold) loses part of its value. The beauty about this is that nothing significant has to happen in the markets for that option to lose value. It's a simple time decay that's kicking in. As time passes, the option you sold becomes cheaper and cheaper until you can finally buy it for a few cents on the dollar.

That's why it's highly lucrative to sell options. You simply sell time to other people who can't stop it.

These four advantages are unique to my option-selling strategy and don't exist in other similar trading strategies. I hope that by now I've got you interested enough to keep on reading. The next two chapters will elaborate on the core fundamentals of my strategy, and how to use my seven-step strategy.

Chapter 4:
My Strategy—General
Guidelines

The previous chapter taught you the basics and the advantages of options selling. It's a language that you must master before you begin to sell options successfully. This chapter will discuss the underlying rationale behind my strategy and the three most important rules of my strategy.

I'll begin with a somewhat odd question—Have you ever dreamed of being the "house" in a casino?

The house is a wonderful position to be in. Gamblers come in and out your door all day long. They all think that they're just a minute away from hitting the jackpot. But as you well know, this rarely happens. What usually happens is that these losing gamblers part ways with their money and leave most, if not all of it, to the house at the end of the day.

There's a reason why the house consistently wins at the expense of these poor gamblers. The house takes only well calculated risks. It has the luxury to pick and choose the bets. In contrast to the gamblers, it's never in a hurry. In other words, it always has an edge. And this edge is the main reason why the house will always make money, whereas gamblers will always lose money.

I liken my strategy in the options market to acting as the house in a crowd of gamblers. It's a very lucrative position to be in. The following example will give you a demonstration on how my strategy really works.

Suppose Joel, your neighbor, owns a great house. It has a great ocean view, a garden, and a marvelous kitchen. You would really like to own that house at some point in time. Now, you know that the market price of your neighbor's house is somewhere in the area of $250,000. That's what Joel will get if he offers it on the market today. But you don't want to pay that sum or anything close to it. You're willing to only pay $200,000 for this beautiful house.

Now, also suppose that Joel approaches you and tells you that he wants to cut a deal with you. The deal goes as follows: He will make you a down payment today if you agree to buy his house from him in a year for $200,000. What Joel is actually asking for is a guarantee from you that you will come up and buy his house from him in a year for $200,000. For this guarantee, he's willing to pay you a handsome fee today.

So what do you think of this deal—will you take it?

Of course you will! I will take this deal every day of the week. I mean, think about it. Joel is actually asking you to buy the house at the price *you wanted in the first place.* In addition, he's also paying you a fat premium just for this obligation. In other words, *Joel is paying you for something you would have done anyway.* And that's the beauty behind my strategy. Now, let's apply this example to the stock market.

Suppose that we're in the month of September and shares of Microsoft are trading for $32 a share. You think that's a *good* price to pay for them, but it isn't a *great* price. Since you're only interested in buying at great prices, you're only willing to pay $30 a share.

The next thing you do is flip through the online option table (I'll show you how to do that later on) and find that many traders are willing to *buy* put options (betting on the stock's decline) at $30 for the month of November. That's only two months down the road (this is September, remember?) And they're also willing to pay you $120 per option.

For you, this is a fantastic win-win scenario. You have already decided that shares of Microsoft are a great value at $30, so you have no problem guaranteeing a purchase at $30. Remember, this event might not even occur to begin with. It's still two months down the road. For this "trouble," you receive an up-front payment of $120 per option.

In November, at expiration date, the share price of Microsoft is revisited. If shares are trading at or above $30, you have no obligation whatsoever, and the premium is yours for free. If, on the other hand, shares trade below the $30 threshold, your obligation kicks in. This means that you will end up buying shares of Microsoft at $30 a share. Again, this is not a big deal because you already decided that paying only $30 a share is a great price. Also, you get to keep the up-front premium, which reduces the overall cost per share to below $30.

To sum it up, you get paid a fee to do something you would have done anyways.

The Insurance Company Model

A different way to think of my strategy is to consider yourself running your own insurance company. An insurance company is a highly lucrative business as long as it writes (sells) clever insurance policies. It must, at all times, evaluate the odds, consider the risk-reward ratio (the risk of loss and the amount of premium), and bet accordingly. In order for your insurance company to remain profitable it must follow three strict rules. I lay them out below.

Rule #1: You only sell options. You don't buy them.

Buying options on a consistent basis is a great recipe for destroying one's portfolio. That's because the odds are always stacked against option *buyers* (remember, we are option *sellers*). You see, option buyers must be right on all three fronts: They must first get the direction (up or down) right. Then, they must be right on the extent of the movement. So if an option buyer purchased an option at the $52 strike, and the stock has gone up but hasn't reached that $52 strike, the trader loses everything.

And lastly, option buyers must also guess the time frame correctly. So if an option buyer purchases an option that expires in November, by November, this option will be delisted from trade and worth precisely zero. Nobody cares that the stock skyrocketed in December. In other words, the option buyer must always give a specific time frame for the stock. Unfortunately for him, time frame is one of the hardest things to guess in the markets. It's on the verge of impossible.

If you put these three obstacles together, you will quickly realize why it's so hard to make money from buying options. And that's why I endorse the exact opposite method—selling options.

Please give this a moment's thought. Buying options is such an extremely difficult task to perform successfully. That's why most options expire worthless. But to every buyer, there's always a seller. So if option buyers consistently *lose* money, guess who consistently *makes* money?

Yes, you guessed it right. It's the option sellers who make money at the expense of gambling option buyers.

Rule #2: You only sell options on stocks that you're willing to buy.

Never ever sell options on stocks that you're not willing to buy. Sometimes, the fat premiums offered to you on risky stocks will appear tempting. You will think that it's worthwhile to sell options on them. It might work the first time around, maybe even the second. But the third time will wipe out your account completely. That's what usually happens to novice option traders. They make it the first time, and then they get wiped out. When that happens, they always blame the system, the SEC, or whoever they first saw on the street that morning. Believe me—I have seen that happen numerous times.

Always keep in mind that when we sell options, we act as an insurance company. That's because we give another party our obligation to buy a stock at a predetermined price by a certain time. Selling options on a risky highflier is like giving a heavy drug addict a life insurance policy. It's a sure recipe for going out of business quickly.

I believe that this is the single most important rule in successful option selling. I can't stress this enough. If you stay away from selling options on risky stocks, you'll do just fine. Don't let that fat, up-front premium make you too greedy. It never ends well.

But now you're probably asking yourself, what are the "right" stocks to sell options on? And which stocks should I avoid at all costs?

I won't fool you on this one. There simply isn't a hard and fast rule to this question. That's because markets are dynamic and valuations change. But what I can and will do is give you my general guidelines of how to pick such stocks. I will also give you my personal list of stocks to sell options on.

I have four basic guidelines on how I choose the companies that I sell options on:

1. The company must be a megacap company *with a market cap of at least $50 billion*. I'm not interested in small-cap companies, because stocks of small-cap companies tend to swing way more than stocks of their larger peers. Remember, we are an insurance company. We're

only interested in safe and steady money. Shooting for the moon isn't for us.

2. The company *cannot operate in a highly volatile business environment*. This means that we'll never sell options on mining companies such as Royal Gold (RGLD) or Barrick Gold (ABX), even though at times they might qualify as excellent investments. The point is that metals and resources in general are hard to predict. So, again, why stick our necks out for the unknown?

3. I will almost always choose *dividend-paying companies that dominate their industries*. What I mean by that is that I will always prefer to sell options on the big names, such as Microsoft (MSFT), Exelon (EXC), or Medtronic (MDT). These are usually the leaders in their fields, be it software, oil, or health care. It has been my experience that stocks of these dividend-paying giants always seem to recover handsomely after every market decline.

4. I will prefer companies that *sell consumer goods and services* over those that don't. Similar to the reasoning I gave in number three above, consumer-goods companies have a strong tendency to weather tough times. They have natural buoyancy. That's because consumers are highly loyal to their brands. Just try and convince a person to switch from Coke or from his Heinz ketchup to a competing brand. You'll see his reaction. This places a virtual floor price on their shares. And that's why I'm more comfortable selling put options

on such stocks. Should I be obligated to buy in shares come expiration day, I will do so willingly and without fear that I might get stuck with the shares forever.

It's important to keep in mind that these four rules aren't exact science. But I always prefer to be approximately right than precisely wrong. These four rules do really work. Sticking with them has definitely increased the size of my bank account, but most importantly has kept me out of harm's way. That's precisely what these four rules can do for you.

My list of favorite companies includes the following: Hershey (HSY), Microsoft (MSFT), Johnson & Johnson (JNJ), Intel (INTC), Apple (AAPL), McDonald's (MCD), Medtronic (MDT), Abbot Labs (ABT), ConocoPhillips (COP), and others. This isn't a closed list. It constantly changes with time, just as markets tend to change. I have attached my own personal list at the appendix of this book for you to take advantage of.

Rule #3: You only sell options when the premium is high enough.

Any well-run insurance company knows how to quantify risk. If it sells silly insurance policies, it might be profitable in the short run. But in the long run, these silly policies will come to run it down to the ground. Since we act as an insurance company, it's imperative to quantify the amount of compensation we receive for our work (selling options). In other words, we will not sell options for too low a premium.

In chapter 2, we discussed volatility and what it means. To make a long story short—fast movements in the price of a stock increase its volatility, and with it, the premium on its options. Since we are option sellers (in contrast to option buyers) we are obviously interested in the highest premium possible. That's because this is the price we will be receiving for the option we sell.

OK. So now you understand that you want to sell options in times of high volatility. But how can you tell when high volatility prevails? It's very simple.

There's a specific financial index that tracks volatility in the markets. I won't burden you with too much information on how this instrument was created, but I will explain exactly how it works. This financial index is called the VIX. It's also widely referred to as "the investor fear gauge," because times of high volatility tend to correspond with times of fear in the markets. VIX is regarded as one of the most widely accepted ways of gauging stock market volatility.

Like any other index or stock, the VIX has a quoted price. You can easily find it on any finance site, like Yahoo! Finance, by clicking "VIX" in the main quote bracket. Theoretically speaking, the VIX ranges between zero and a hundred. But that's only in theory. Under very extreme conditions (like the 2008 crisis) the VIX hits eighty. In times of high complacency, the VIX has a reading of ten or below.

I use VIX as a gauge to guide me when to sell and when not to sell options, by following the rules below.

1. **VIX less than twenty**: I refrain from selling options when the VIX reading is below twenty. This means that the market is complacent and that I'm not getting enough compensation for my options. I won't try to force the market to pay me if it doesn't want to. I'll stay on the sidelines.

2. **VIX greater than fifty**: I always sell options when the VIX reading is above fifty. This means that the market is in a very pessimistic mood. Volatility is sky high and so are option premiums. I will be highly compensated for selling options, so that's exactly what I'll do.

3. **VIX between twenty and fifty**: I will sell options from time to time, depending on the specific stock, when the VIX reading is between twenty and fifty. This is the normal VIX range that the market is in. It means that times are ripe for selling options, but you have to cherry-pick the most appropriate stocks to sell options on. This is a good environment for option sellers. You can make a great living from it.

To sum it all up, the VIX is an important gauge that gives us a great clue when it's a good time to be an options seller and when it isn't. Make sure you stick with the rules.

Chapter 5:
My Seven-Step Strategy—
Step by Step

In chapters 3 and 4, I introduced you to my strategy. You learned the basic guidelines and the underlying rationale behind my theory by using some exam ples and metaphors. I hope that by now you're convinced that my strategy does make perfect sense. And if used sensibly, it can easily beat any other trading strategy that you might know.

This chapter discusses the nuts and bolts of my strategy and how it actually makes money. As promised, I will guide you step by step in how it works.

Step #1: Identifying the Stock That You Want to Sell Options On

We've already agreed that we won't sell options on highfliers, no matter how high a premium is offered to us. That's the most important rule of my strategy. If you violate it, you will lose your edge and become just like any other option-buying gambler. Your account will also look like his—empty and penniless. Since you've purchased this book to become wealthy, you will always refrain from selling options on highfliers. Agreed?

Great, now the highfliers are out the window. But how will you choose the stocks that you *do* want to sell options on? I've got two quick rules for you.

Rule #1

Consult my personal stock list. I gave you a little taste of it in the previous chapter. You can find my complete personal list in the appendix of this book. This list consists of companies that lead their industries, pay high dividends, an d tend to increase their per-share earnings over time. This is our favorite list because it greatly reduces the risk in guaranteeing their share price. That's why I personally prefer to sell options on Coca-Cola or McDonald's but never on companies such as Tesla Motors (TSLA).

Once you become more experienced, you'll be able to create your own list of favorite stocks to sell options on. So, for example, if you are highly familiar with the dining industry, you might decide that you wish to sell options on companies like Dunkin' Donuts (DNKN) or Chipotle Mexican Grill (CMG). That's because you know these are industry-leading companies trading at a fair price, and you don't mind owning them. You will develop this type of skill as you practice my strategy.

Rule #2

Check on the company's value metrics. It's been my experience that selling put options on cheap stocks tends to be much more rewarding than selling puts on stocks that have gone up a lot in price in proportion to their earnings.

The easiest and most accessible way to check whether or not a stock is cheap enough is to look up its price/earnings (P/E). What this metric does is divide the company's share price by its earnings per share. The higher the reading, the more expensive the stock is.

The easiest way for you to check the P/E reading of your specific stock is to go to Yahoo! Finance. Then, type the symbol of your company in the upper-left bracket. The P/E reading will appear at the center of the screen right below the "market cap."

The optimal cases are when the stocks of companies from our list above trade at a P/E of 12x or lower. This places them in the utmost cheap category, and this increases our chances of winning. I also sell options on stocks that trade at a P/E range of 12x–20x, depending on the circumstances and the general market conditions. What I don't do, though, is sell options on stocks with a P/E higher than 20x. Such a high P/E is usually a sign of pricing trouble. The stock's price has been bid up by overwhelming optimists, and I don't want to take part in this fiasco.

Keep in mind that this isn't a perfect tool. Sometimes, cheap stocks decline in price and become even cheaper. But I always prefer to be approximately right than precisely wrong. By judging the P/E of a company prior to selling options on it, we place the odds in our favor.

In conclusion, the ideal stock to sell options on will be a company that belongs to our predetermined list of market leaders and is trading at a cheap enough price.

Step #2: Getting the Timing Right

Successful timing is a combination of both general market events and company-specific events. When you search for convenient market conditions for option selling, look no further than the VIX. As I explained in chapter 4, when the VIX has a reading below twenty, stay out of the market and stop selling options. It means that the market doesn't reward us sufficiently for our underwriting activities.

On the other hand, when the VIX has a reading above fifty, you can sell options almost indiscriminately. That's an extreme situation, and you can take advantage of it. In most cases, though, reality lies somewhere between these two extremes. With the VIX ranging between twenty and fifty, you can and should sell options, but you also have to cherry-pick your candidates.

In simple words, the VIX serves as the market's barometer and as such, determines for us the proper market conditions for option selling. Our next stage is to look for specific company-oriented events to give us an indication that now is the right time to sell options *on that specific stock.*

When I look for specific, company-related news, what I'm actually looking for is a "trigger event" in one of the stocks on our list. A trigger event is any market event that creates a substantial negative shock in the market price of the stock. For example, back in September 2013, Apple stock dropped more than 5 percent in a single day after announcing a launch of its cheaper iPhone—the model 5C. Another example is Microsoft dropping by as much as 12 percent in a single day (Wow!) after the company announced some disappointing results for the second quarter of 2013.

The underlying rationale behind this rule is simple. It has been my experience that any major daily swing (anything above 5 percent) in megacap stocks is a result of pure panic. In almost all cases, this panic selling relaxes in the next couple of days, and the share price reverts back to its former self in a few short weeks.

So, how do we spot trigger events ahead of time?

Nothing is sure in the markets, but trigger events tend to correspond with major corporate announcements. So, for example, earnings season is naturally a great time to sell options on companies from our list. It's so common for a great company to miss earnings by a cent or two here and there. This ignites a panic selling with no real grounds to it. In a couple of short weeks, well—the price is back to normal as if nothing had happened. *So, earnings season is a good time to pay close attention to our list of stocks.*

Another noteworthy milestone is the release of important macro-reports, such as the report on PC sales. Such reports tend to have a strong immediate impact on companies that are involved in that field. So, for example, a strong drop in PC sales might trigger a large drop in the price of Intel, which sells microprocessor chips to PC companies. Similar to the price swings around earnings reports, such swings also tend to be short lived. Everyone panics and then forgets. That's how mankind has been programmed. We're here to take advantage of that and resist this type of group thinking by the herds.

In conclusion, the ideal timing to sell options on stocks is when the VIX is above twenty and *the company's stock has just experienced a short-term negative shock.*

Step #3: The Optimal Strike Price

As I've explained in Chapter 2, options vary in their strike prices. For each company and for each time frame (see below), you can choose from a large set of strike prices. For example, Coca-Cola is currently trading for $40. You can sell options at the $38 strike, the $40 strike, the $42 strike, or any other strike price that you can imagine.

In order to choose the optimal strike price for your options, you need to learn a bit about option pricing. If you don't like to think too much about this, feel free to skip this explanation and go straight to the rule I set below. This in no way will affect your trading as long as you stick with the rule I have set below. But if you wish to gain a better understanding of the world of options, the following explanation is just for you.

Some Insight on Options Pricing

When choosing the optimal strike price for the options we sell, we first must understand how options are priced to begin with. After all, there's always a reason why an option trades at a specific price. The price of any option has two main components—the intrinsic value component and the time component.

The Intrinsic Value Component

This component is embedded in the option price, and is represented by the *difference between the strike price and the prevailing market price of the stock.* Say, for example, that shares of Coca-Cola are trading at $40 and you sell a put option on Coca-Cola at a strike price of $35. This means that you've got an intrinsic value of $5 embedded in the option already ($40 minus $35). It makes perfect sense. Since you're obligated to buy shares at $35, you're currently $5 ahead of your obligation. That's because the current market price is $5 higher than the price at which your obligation is triggered.

The same rule applies if the strike price of your option is higher than the market price. For example, shares of Coca-Cola are trading at $40 and you sell a put option on Coca-Cola at a strike price of $42. The strike price that triggers your obligation is *higher* than the current market price. What do you think is the intrinsic value of the option under this scenario?

You guessed it right. It's zero, nothing. When you sell a put option with a strike price that's higher than the current market price—you have no intrinsic value.

In other words, intrinsic value is the amount option traders would get if a trade closed that day. It's how far an option is in the money. If a stock is trading at $33, the $32 call options have $1 in intrinsic value...no matter the expiration date or how much the total option premium is.

The Time Value Component

The unique thing about options is that they are set to expire sometime in the future. If they were set to expire right now, for example, there would be no point in using options because the market can tell us the exact price quote of the security.

This uncertainty and opportunity going well into the future is considered the time value of the option. After all, anything can happen in a few short months, and no one knows for sure at what price shares of Coca-Cola will trade three months down the road. Time value is the price option buyers have to pay for the potential to profit. The further away the option is from expiration, the higher the chance that the option will become profitable. So you'll find more time value "baked in" to the premium.

Time value can be quantified. It could go as high as tens of dollars per option for options that expire in fifteen or twenty-four months. And it could go as low as a few cents for options that expire next week. By now you have realized that options that expire tomorrow, for instance, have no time value left in them. Time value is whatever is left over after you subtract the intrinsic value out of an option premium. So let's say those same $32 calls are trading for $2.50. With the stock at $33, the call option has $1.50 in time value. (That's the $2.50 premium minus the $1 in intrinsic value.)

There's one secret thing you should know about time value in options: it doesn't evaporate in a linear way. Let me explain this statement. As time passes by (it always does...), the time value component in the option is slowly decaying. That's because, all being equal, an option with five months to expiration is more expensive than the same option two months later. It makes perfect sense. But the thing is that as expiration day gets closer, the time value is eroding more aggressively. So much so that in the two weeks prior to expiration, there's little to no time value left.

You'd be surprised to know that not many option buyers are aware of that phenomenon. This makes their odds of winning even slimmer. There's nothing like a decaying time value to destroy the price of options. As far as I know, no person to date has successfully stopped time. This, of course, plays right to our hands as option sellers. Once we sell the options, we are delighted to see their price decline over time, giving us the chance to buy them and close the position for a handsome profit. In simple words, time value is the compensation for future uncertainty.

OK. So now you understand how options are priced and what intrinsic value and time value mean in regard to options.

If you've read my book carefully, you might think that I forgot to mention a third factor that affects the pricing of options. You probably remember that I previously mentioned volatility and the effect that volatility has on the price of options. It's very true. The more volatile a share is, the higher the premium is on its options. Nevertheless, I do not consider volatility to be a permanent, stable component in the pricing of options. Sometimes it's there, and sometimes it isn't. That's why I only mention the two stable components (intrinsic value and time) that determine the price of options.

That's the end of this short pricing theory on options. Now let's get back to our main topic which is to how we pick and choose an optimal strike price.

It has been my experience that selling put options with too high a strike price (out of the money) is simply too risky for me despite the higher up-front premium that I might receive. Please give this a moment's thought.

If shares of Coca-Cola are now trading for $40, why should we commit to buy shares (in three months) for $42 a share? If we make such commitment, we are actually counting on some price appreciation between today and three months from now. This is far from certain, and it certainly increases our degree of risk.

On the other hand, selling options with too low a strike price (in the money) is simply not rewarding enough in terms of return on our capital. Let's return to the same example as above. Shares of Coca-Cola are still trading at $40. We can certainly commit to buy shares three months from now at a strike price of $35. On the face of it, it's a great deal because the risk is so small. The problem, of course, is that so is the reward. You can't make real money by guaranteeing such a low share price relative to the market price. There has to be some correlation. Going back to our example, we will prefer to sell options on Coca-Cola shares at a strike price of $40 or $39—not higher than $40 and not lower than $39, no matter how tempting the up-front premium is. In other words, we will not sell OTM put options.

In conclusion, we will always sell options at or around the strike price. It really doesn't have to be exactly on the cent. One dollar more or one dollar less is still fine.

Step #4: Choosing the Optimal Time Frame

I'll start by saying that selling options isn't an exact science. So there isn't really a wrong time frame, just like there isn't a right time frame. You can sell options that expire twelve months from now, or you can sell options that expire in a week. Everything is available to you.

But my experience has taught me that the best way to maximize your return on invested capital is to sell options that expire between two and four months from now. So if we're in September 2013, you want to be looking to sell options that expire in November 2013, December 2013, January 2014, or February 2014 at the latest.

If you sell options with a shorter time frame than two months, your return will be eroded by fees and commissions. If you sell options with too long a time frame (such as a year), you will do fine, but not great. I will illustrate this statement with the following example:

In most cases, if you sell options on Microsoft that expire a year from today, you can make about 8 percent annualized on your invested capital. If, on the other hand, you choose to sell three-month-long options four times a year, you can easily generate 12 percent and sometimes more. That's because a three-month option can give you a return of about 3 percent. Repeat this four times a year and you'll be looking at 12 percent return on your capital.

Why is this situation possible, you ask?

Selling year-long options once a year isn't a difficult task, and that's why the compensation is good but not great. But traders who are willing to put in the effort, check the options table, and sell option four times a year will be rewarded with a handsome return that is about 50 percent higher than if they were to sell options only once a year.

This doesn't mean that we'll only be selling options with an expiration period of three months. The market is dynamic, and so we'll take advantage of every mispricing mistake that we can spot. We'll always aspire to achieve the most optimal return on our capital and avoid suboptimal returns. Always remember, we're the house, and the gamblers come to us. We get to choose which options we sell to them, at what strike price and for how long. Because the odds are tilted to favor us (most options expire worthless), we'll make money at the expense of these gamblers.

In conclusion, the optimal time frame to sell options on is around three months.

Step #5: Calculating Your Potential Profit on a Trade

Before we place an actual trade, we must consider the odds and make sure that they're stacked in our favor. Put differently, we always want the probability to favor us. If the word "probability" scares you, simply replace it with the word "opportunity." That's how I see things in life in general, and in trading in specific.

Let's say that we've picked a great stock to sell options on. We also chose the time frame and the strike price. This is shaping up to be a great opportunity. But *how* great, exactly? We always need to compute our expected return on capital *before* we actually place a trade. As always, we'll use a real trade example to illustrate how we derive our expected return.

As of this writing (September 2013), shares of Intel are trading at $23.44. My next step now is to flip to the option table on Yahoo! Finance to check the price quotes for options on Intel (just click the "Options" bracket on the toolbar to the left).

I fast-forward to my favorite time bracket, which is normally three months ahead. This gets me to the expiration date for the month of December. Specifically, these options will expire on December 21, 2013. My next step is to look up the quotes for my favorite strike price. Since Intel is trading at $23.44, my natural choice would be to choose the $23 strike price. By now, we have followed up on steps 1 through 4 in my guideline.

I now check the price quote for this series of options. The quote on the screen reads $0.93 right next to the $23 strike price bracket. This means that option sellers will get paid $0.93 to sell an option for a single share of Intel. But since option contracts only trade at multiples of a hundred, the more practical way to look at this would be that option sellers will be paid $93 to sell an option for $2,300 worth of Intel stock. All we did was multiply the previous strike price ($23) and the cost ($0.93) by a hundred. Everything else remained equal.

Now let's do some simple third-grade math. We will receive a payment of $93 for a future obligation of $2,300. This means that the gross return on our trade is 4 percent (93 divided by 2,300, times one hundred). This trade will last from September 2013 to December 2013, a total of three months.

This makes the annualized return on our trade a fantastic 16 percent (4 percent times four). Not bad, right?

But it gets even better. Here comes a time to rethink the comparison that I previously made between my strategy and the way insurance companies operate. You see, the real beauty behind the money generation of insurance companies lies in the float (or the premium). A float is what insurance companies receive in consideration for their current obligation to insure a future event. Now, this event might not even occur, but the payment (the up-front premium) stays in their pockets nonetheless.

Let's go back to my strategy. The possibility that we might be obligated to buy Intel shares three months from now is no sure event. In fact, it's not even likely that this event will happen. It will only happen should Intel shares trade below the $23 threshold that we set. In other words, we don't have to invest anything today. It's a future obligation on our part. If it happens, we're fine with that. But the most important part here is that no one's asking us *to invest or put down any money right now*. We're just like an insurance company in that sense.

We will only need to set aside 20 percent of the value of our obligation (in this case it's $460). This money isn't going anywhere. It's called a margin requirement, and it's sitting in cash right in our trading account. That's what our broker is going to be asking us to set aside just so he can be sure that we don't run away with our obligation to some distant place on the globe.

Since we only have to set aside the amount of $460, and by the end of three months we will make $93, our return on investment (or return on cash) is a staggering 20 percent (93 divided by 460 times one hundred) in a short three months.

If we repeat this trade four times a year, we're looking at an annual return on cash of 80 percent.

I understand that this seems peculiarly high to you, and that you might even think that I'm deluding you or misinforming you in some way. That's just not true. My strategy is simple yet very powerful. There's absolutely nothing in this strategy that you can't implement from your home computer by using a standard Internet connection. It's as simple and as powerful as that. Yes, you can make 16 percent a year on your investments or 80 percent a year on your cash.

In conclusion, to compute our return on investment we divide the option premium by the total obligation and multiply that number by a hundred.

Step #6: Drawing a Risk-Reward Scenario

Let's say we've picked a great stock to sell options on, and that we also chose the optimal strike price and the optimal time frame. We've also computed our potential profit (step 5), and now comes the time for step 6. In this step, we will try and draw all the potential outcomes of our trade. This will give us a better visualization going forward. For simplicity, I'll base this step on the same example we just used in step 4.

Just to refresh your memory, we're now about to sell put options on Intel at the $23 strike price that expire in December 2013. We will be paid an up-front payment of $93 for each option contract (one hundred shares) we sell. This payment will obligate us to buy Intel shares in the open market in December, should their price drop below the predetermined $23.

How Our Trade Plays Out

There are three different scenarios that can play out on expiration day in December 2013:

1. **Share price of Intel is greater than $23**: You get to pocket the premium and have no obligation.

2. **Share price of Intel equals $23**: You get to pocket the premium and have no obligation.

3. **Share price of Intel is less than $23**: You get to pocket the premium, but you will also be obligated to buy shares at the predetermined price of $23. Your effective buying price per share will end up being $22.07 ($23 minus $0.93). That's because you were initially paid a premium per share of $0.93. Since this is an excellent price to pay for the shares, you should be fine with that obligation.

These are the *only* three scenarios that can happen on the day of expiration in the month of December. Note that in two of these three scenarios, you get to walk with the up-front premium and have no obligation whatsoever. This is another aspect of how the odds are stacked in your favor. *Before you even place the trade, you know that in two out of three scenarios - you walk out a clear winner.* Most traders would give up their house for such remarkable odds.

By drawing out the three scenarios for each option trade, you can clear out all the fog. Nothing remains uncertain. Remember, you're the insurance company. You just wrote a very clever and lucrative insurance policy whose outcomes are laid out before you. You will always know the odds and never be surprised.

In conclusion, in order to draw the risk-reward scenario, you must write down the (only) three possible outcomes— shares above the strike price, shares at the strike price, and shares below the strike price.

Step #7: Diversification

Novice option traders tend to make large, infrequent bets. They place all their capital on a single horse. But skilled option traders know better than that. They diversify their bets and they make frequent bets every three months or so.

Although the odds are heavily in our favor before we initiate a trade, diversification is an important tool. In practice, and as you become more seasoned, I usually recommend maintaining at least three different open positions on three different sectors and with three different time frames.

For example, you can have an open position on Intel that expires in May, another open position on Medtronic that expires in June, and a third open position on McDonald's that expires in July. That is what I call a balanced approach. That's because at any given time, you are exposed to companies from three different sectors (microprocessors, health care, and restaurants) and with varying expiration dates (May, June, July). This greatly reduces the risk of a sudden obligation coming due on all fronts simultaneously.

These are the seven steps that are the cornerstones of my strategy. Learn them, remember them, and then practice them in real market conditions. This seven-step program is the key to your financial success in the markets.

Chapter 6:
Your Obligation Is Due

In most cases (more than 85 percent of all trades), we get to walk away from the trade with a nice premium in our pockets, and more importantly, we're obligation free. Put differently, most trades don't end with us having to actually buy the shares we initially committed to. But from time to time, shares that we sold put options on drop in price and our obligation becomes due. This chapter will discuss what you should do if your obligation becomes due by expiration day.

Suppose we sold these put options on Intel at the $23 strike price back in September. We decided to sell two options for which we received an immediate up-front payment of $186 ($93 times two). Today is December 18, and the expiration day for the options is December 21, only three days away.

Suppose also that shares of Intel are now trading at around $22. This is one dollar *below* the price we promised to guarantee ($23). This means that in three days we will be obligated to go out and purchase two hundred shares (we sold two options, remember?) for $23 a share.

This is a classic scenario of our obligation becoming due. It doesn't happen very often, but it does happen from time to time. My personal trading diary indicates that in less than 15 percent of all cases I end up with an obligation. In all other cases, I'm simply left with my up-front payment, free of any obligation.

The most important notion to understand here is that my strategy doesn't regard such scenarios as incidents or mistakes. An insurance company hasn't made a mistake if a certain percentage of its policies end up with a payment obligation. It's simply a normal course of business. Lucky for us, and contrary to an insurance company, there's no need for us to go out and pay someone in cash. All we have to do is purchase an asset (shares) that are worth owning.

After you devote some time to this idea, you will become almost indifferent to a scenario whereby your obligation is due by the expiration date. Basically, it isn't such a big deal. But this in no way means we have lost money on this specific trade. Below are two trading methods to handle such a scenario.

Method #1: Cover Your Obligation

I'll begin to illustrate method #1 by stating that this is not my favorite way. In theory, it shouldn't be used at all, except for situations when you absolutely get scared out of your position and decide to "put down your chips." If you stick with the original board plan, there's no reason for you to implement method #1. That's why I refer to this method as a "last minute" rescue plan to be used in radical cases only.

Our initial obligation was first created when we sold the Intel options back in September. This obligation can be replaced, or covered, by exercising the exact opposite transaction. We can "buy to close" these options.

This means that if we "sold to open" two options in September, we would now (December) buy to close these same two options. Once we do that, there's no pending obligation any more. But at what price, you might be asking yourself? That's a good question.

Let's go back to the basics and try and figure out the estimated price for our options today. As we previously learned, the price of options is comprised of two factors: intrinsic value and time value. Assuming that shares of Intel are now trading at $22, this implies that our options have an intrinsic value of $1 (our strike price minus current price). Regarding the time value—there's none. If you recall, I previously explained how time value is easily eroded, especially as options come near their expiration date. With only three days to expiration date, the time value is nonexistent.

The bottom line of this calculation is that each of our options is currently trading at or about $100 ($1 times one hundred shares). This means that we are down $200 on our position ($1 per share times two hundred shares). Since we initially received an up-front payment of $186, we are down only $14 on this transaction as a whole. That's not too great but it isn't too bad either.

But again, this isn't my preferred way of dealing with a situation when the stock price goes against us. Nonetheless, it's still a tool. Keep it in your arsenal.

Method #2: Exercise Your Obligation

My second, and preferred, method is to exercise our obligation. By that, I mean to actually buy the *shares* at the predetermined price ($23), rather than simply cover our obligation by buying the *options*.

As you recall, the fundamental principle behind my strategy is to only buy stocks of companies that you want to own, at a price you're willing to pay. Going back to the drawing board—we initially agreed to pay $23 per share of Intel. This shouldn't change now. We understand that this price decline is mostly attributed to momentary dislike by Mr. Market. This dislike might disappear overnight.

In practice, we'll wait until expiration day passes. Then, we'll instruct our broker to buy us two hundred shares of Intel at $23 a share for a total capital layout of $4,600. This satisfies our obligation to the market. My experience has taught me that by sticking to shares of world-dominating businesses we'll do just fine. That's because the high-dividend payouts tend to support the share price in good and bad times alike. By this I mean that the share price usually climbs back to $23 very soon. This leaves us with no obligation and a nice premium in our pockets.

Chapter 7:
How to Turn a Losing Trade into a Winner

The previous chapter ended with the possibility that our obligation is due. In that case, we must come up with the money and buy the number of shares we previously committed to buy. At times, we might book a temporary loss on the trade.

In this chapter, I will discuss a secret trick that turns almost any unprofitable trade back to being profitable.

The trick is to sell covered call options on the underlying shares that you now own.

Selling a covered call creates a similar obligation to selling a put option. Remember that when we sell a put option, we guarantee a "floor price" to the stock, so if it drops below this threshold, we will step up and buy shares. Conversely, when we sell a call option, we create an obligation to transfer our shares if the price goes up above a predetermined "ceiling price." Let's use the example below to shed some light on this trick.

Suppose we own one hundred shares of McDonald's that we bought a year ago for $85. Let's also assume that the stock has been treading water for the past six months, thereby making us zero return on our money. What we can do is sell a call option at the $88 strike price that expires three months from today. By selling the call option, we instantly earn an up-front payment, just like we did when we sold the put option on Intel. This payment also creates an obligation. If, and only if, shares of McDonald's *trade above $88* come expiration date, we will be obligated to "give away" our shares.

Selling a call option is a mirror trade to selling a put option. When we sell a put option, we are obligated to *buy shares* if the share price drops *below* a certain price. When we sell a call option, we are obligated to *sell shares* (that we already own) if the share price goes *above* a certain price.

Now let's return to our original trade. It's now December 2013, and we are the proud owners of two hundred Intel shares as a result of the put options we sold back in September. In order to implement my trick, we need to go out and sell two call options on these very stocks. Since the stock price is now $22, whereas we were "put" the stock at $23, we will now turn around and sell two call options (one for every one hundred shares that we have) at the $23 strike price. We'll pick our favorite time frame of three months. For this, we will receive an up-front payment of roughly $160 ($80 per option contract).

There are three different scenarios that can play out on expiration day in March 2014:

1. **Share price of Intel is less than $23**: You get to pocket the premium and have no obligation. You can now sell another round of covered calls for the June expiration date, and earn another fee.

2. **Share price of Intel equals $23**: You get to pocket the premium and have no obligation. You can now sell another round of covered calls for the June expiration date, and earn another fee.

3. **Share price of Intel is greater than $23**: You get to pocket the premium, but you will also be obligated to give away your shares at the predetermined price of $23.

Under scenarios one and two, we have no obligation to give away our Intel shares. This means that we get to keep our $160 (from the calls we sold), the $186 (from the puts we sold), *plus* we also get to keep the shares. This brings our total trade balance to a positive $140 ($160 plus $180 minus $200). What we will now do is sell another series of

June 2014 call options on our shares at the same $23 strike price.

Under scenario three, we must give away our Intel shares. This means that we get to keep our $160 (from the calls we sold) and the $186 (from the puts we sold). In return, our shares are taken away from us.

Now please give this a moment's thought. Even though our initial trade (selling the put) didn't turn out a winner, our follow-up trade (selling the call) placed it squarely back into the profitable zone. It might take us three more months, but our trade will be profitable in more than 92 percent of cases according to my own personal trading diary.

My strategy beats any other option-trading strategy out there.

Chapter 8:
How to Place and How to Close a Trade

From the very start of this book, I have repeatedly emphasized that this book isn't meant to remain theoretical. This is a very practical guide on how to make a living by selling equity options. And that's why the goal of this chapter is to walk you through the specifics of how to place and how to close a trade. These are the precise instructions you should give your broker.

How to Place a Trade

Since we refrain from buying options, our trade will always be initiated by an order to "sell to open" options. Such an order will look like this: **"Sell to open the December 2013 put options on Intel at the $23 strike price."**

Always make sure that your order begins with a sell to open instruction. Then, you have to make sure that it includes all the specifics we have talked about. It must contain the expiration date (December 2013), the type of option (put), the company's name (Intel) and the strike price ($23). That's how a complete order looks.

Sometimes we wish to sell options on stocks that we already own. In this case, we don't sell put options but call options (refresh your memory with chapter 7 above). In such a case, the order will look like this: "**Sell to open the December 2013 call options on Intel at the $23 strike price.**"

This order will obligate us to give away our shares of Intel if, and only if, shares of Intel trade above $23 come expiration day.

These are the only two forms of orders that we will use to place a trade. *We never begin a trade with a "buy to open" type of order.* That's an important rule.

How to Close a Trade

Whereas a trade can be initiated by using one form of order and one form only, a trade can be *closed* in numerous ways.

Method #1: Covering Your Obligation

Whether you wish to cover (close) your pending obligation on expiration day or way before it, you'll use the following order type: "**Buy to close the December 2013 put options on Intel at the $23 strike price.**"

Remember, this time you are terminating your pending obligation. Since your obligation has initially begun with a sale of options, then it will be closed by buying the very same options you previously sold. Once you perform a buy in of the options, your obligation is terminated and finalized.

The same is, of course, true for covering your obligation on a call option. If you wish to refrain from a situation where you must give away your shares, you must terminate the obligation by buying the call options you initially sold. You do this by using the following order: "**Buy to close the December 2013 call options on Intel at the $23 strike price.**"

By using the above order and buying the calls you initially sold, you're now covered, obligation free.

Method #2: Exercising Your Obligation

If your obligation is due on expiration day and you wish to realize it rather than cover it, you need to step up and buy the shares you initially committed to buy. You'll use the following order: "**Buy two hundred shares of Intel at $23 a share.**"

Remember, in this case the share price ended up lower than the strike price we initially committed to. That's why we have to step up and exercise our obligation to buy shares. Since we initially sold two put options on Intel, we now must buy two hundred shares of Intel.

If your trade began by selling call options, and now is expiration day, and your obligation to give away your shares is due—there's no need for any special order. Your two hundred Intel shares will disappear from your trading account after clearing and settlement take place, which is usually two days after expiration day.

Method #3: No Obligation

Suppose that you sold put options or call options a few months ago. Also suppose that we're now on expiration day, and the share price is out of the money. This means that you have no obligation to buy in shares if you sold put options, and you have no obligation to give away your shares if you sold call options.

What type of order will you use?

The answer is no order. There's absolutely nothing you should do on expiration day if your obligation isn't due.

You keep the up-front premium that was paid to you when you initially sold the options, whether puts or calls, obligation free.

In conclusion, this chapter described in detail all the relevant orders that you need to use when you implement my strategy. There are no more tools that you need.

Chapter 9:
The Alpha of Technical Analysis

In this chapter I'll explain in detail how technical analysis can greatly assist you in implementing my strategy.

Wikipedia defines technical analysis as a "methodology for forecasting the direction of prices through the study of past market data, primarily price and volume." In contrast to the fundamental methodology that checks conventional metrics like earnings and profit margins, the technical methodology is based solely on price action.

The basic assumption underlying technical analysis is that all the relevant information is already embedded in the stock price. What's left to figure out is where the price is likely to go next from there.

Many investors and traders alike tend to dismiss technical analysis altogether and refer to it as some "miraculous mumbo jumbo" that cannot make you money. It has been my experience that they are partly right, but only partly.

I strongly discourage anyone from attempting to make a living in the markets by exploiting the merits of technical analysis. It used to work pretty well in the 1970s, when only a handful of traders had access to computerized trading and a sophisticated graph system. Today, these tools are far from scarce, which is precisely why technical analysis has lost its edge.

But this doesn't mean that technical analysis is futile. My strategy greatly benefits from the use of technical analysis. Specifically, we take advantage of this analysis in determining the *optimal strike price* at which we decide to sell our equity options.

Some Background on Technical Tools

You've got so many technical tools out there like Bollinger Bands, oscillators, and various MACDs. The bad news is that elaborating on them is way beyond the scope of this book. The good news is that you don't really need to learn about them to use my strategy properly. I will now teach you precisely what you need to know.

We'll begin by looking at the dark green chart below. This chart shows the price performance of Microsoft stock in the period of April 2013 up until October 2013. It's called a six-month chart. If you wish, you can choose almost any time frame, but I've learned that the six-month gives me enough information and yet doesn't overburden me with too much data.

The left column gives you an indication of the daily trading volume in the shares, while the column to the right gives you an indication of the price per share. At the bottom of the graph you can see indication of the time period in months and days. In between the two columns, you've got price bars.

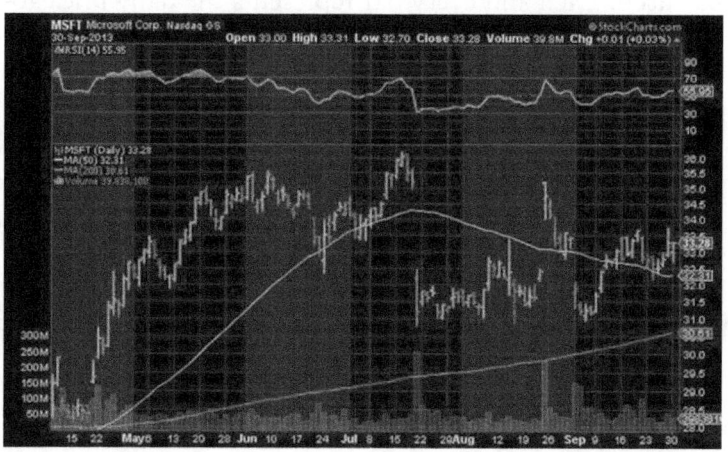

The bars that you see in the graph represent the daily price action of the stock. Each bar represents a single trading day, from open to close. Green-colored bars represent up days while the red-colored bars represent down days. As you can see from the graph, roughly 70 percent of the trading days in the period were red (down) days while about 30 percent were green (up) days. You can also see that in the course of this six-month time frame, the stock price of Microsoft climbed from around $28.50 to $33.28.

Each price bar has two "handles"—one on each of its sides. The handle to its left represents the stock price at the open, and the handle to its right represents the stock price at the close. But the most important thing to look at is the bar itself. Each and every bar represents the daily price action—from peak to trough. Hence, the upper part of each bar represents the day's high, while the lower part of each bar represents the day's low. During the trading day, the stock price swings between the high and the low.

You should always consider these two extremes—the high and the low of each bar. That's because on each and every trading day you've got a crowd of buyers and a crowd of sellers. It's a bidding war. By observing the high and the low of each day you can tell how aggressive and excited buyers were, and how desperate and fearful sellers were.

By looking at the high-low price graph over a six-month period, you can gather a lot of information on the persistence of buyers and sellers for this stock. In particular, you can figure out at which price sellers would step in and begin to sell aggressively, and at which price buyers would jump in and begin to buy in loads. This is extremely useful information.

By following up on the action represented by the price bars, we correspond with one of the most important concepts of technical analysis—to always ride the trend and never resist it. By following the trend, whether up or down, you gain advantage of the short-term momentum.

How My Strategy Uses
Technical Analysis

Now that you've learned the basics of technical analysis, we'll go on and use it to our benefit. My strategy uses the information from price bars to optimize our decision on the proper strike price for the option. Our main consideration when choosing a strike price is not to shoot for the moon, but also not to shoot too low and be paid too low a premium.

By reviewing the six-month price action of the stock, we can say, with a relatively high probability, at which point buyers will step in and bid up the price. In other words, we can make an intelligent guesstimate on the floor price of the stock. This floor price will protect us when we sell put options on the stock.

Let's use the Microsoft six-month price graph for an example. Upon reviewing the graph, we can tell that the $31 price threshold serves as a line of support. That's because the lower ends of the price bars stop at that price and create a floor. Put differently, every time sellers had the upper hand pushing the stock down, they never managed to push it lower than the $31 line. It's an important line of support.

As a general rule, we'll never sell options at a strike price that is lower than the floor price in the graph.

If you follow the graph closely, you'll note that recently another floor price was established. The $32.31 price also serves as a line of support. That's because on September 23 sellers tried and failed to push the price lower. So now the lower end of this bar (at $32.31) serves as another line of support.

In order to optimize our option's strike price, we'll almost always choose the most recent support line that has been tested and found reliable. In this case, it means $32.31. Since strike prices are only denominated in round numbers, we'll use the $32 strike price as the most efficient strike price—one that will reward us with a nice premium *and* protect us from the downside.

I want to give you another example to make sure you've got this. Below is a six-month chart of Apple stock. What do you think is the optimal strike price for the options we sell?

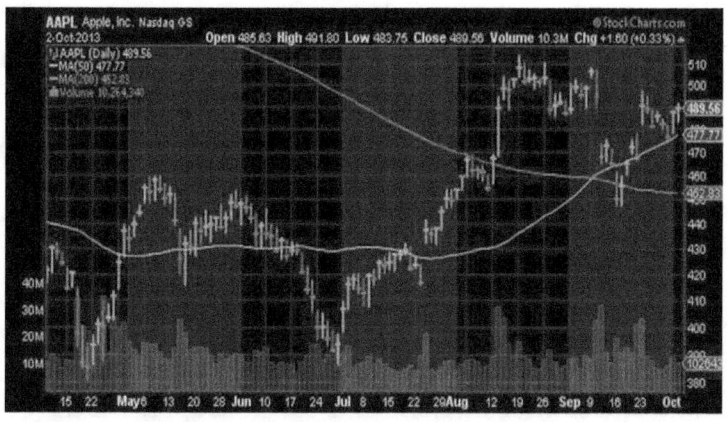

That's right! The answer is $478. The most recent support line stood at $477. From that point, buyers quickly appeared, and the price shot up to $489. Also worth mentioning is another support line at the $452 price, although the latter will reward us with a much smaller premium.

How to Create Your Own Visual Graph

Looking up a stock chart is extremely easy. All you have to do is go to the free website Stockcharts.com, and inside the main bracket, insert the stock ticker.

For ease of reading, change the type of chart from "Candlesticks" to "OHLC Bars" in the "Chart Attributes" section below. Also change the color scheme from "Default" to "Dark Green," and you're all set to go. The chart of your favorite stock will appear. Now follow the bars on your chart and try and spot the most recent support lines over the past three months or so.

To sum it all up, trading analysis should never be used as a stand-alone tool. In our case, it isn't. We have a well-established trading strategy supported by fundamental reasoning, to which we also add a component from the world of technical analysis. This balanced approach can be highly rewarding.

Chapter 10:
A Real Trade from Start to Finish

My goal with this book will be complete only when you become a successful option seller who's able to consistently earn a monthly income from selling options.

In this chapter, I'll walk you hand in hand through a real, live trade. The purpose of this chapter is for you to see how my seven-step strategy is implemented under real market conditions.

The trade that I discuss below lasted for three months—from June 2013 until expiration day on September 2013.

1) My first step was to keep an eye on our list of stock candidates. One of my favorite stocks on the list is

Microsoft, which has been treading water recently, going nowhere but sideways despite its massive market dominance. At the time, Microsoft had been trading at a measly P/E of only 10x. This places it squarely in the very cheap category under rule #2. It seemed ripe to sell options on, but I knew that I had some more homework to complete before I sold options on this giant, undervalued stock.

2) The second step was to make sure that the timing was right. Specifically, I needed to check that both market conditions *and* company-specific conditions were right. When I checked the VIX for market conditions, I got a reading above twenty. That's pretty good considering that the stock market has been on a continuous bull market in 2013, and so the VIX spent most of its time well under fifteen. Regarding Microsoft, the media has been talking nonstop about the declining PC sales. Many pundits on CNBC haven't been able to stop talking about the gloomy future for Microsoft. These are my favorite conditions.

3) My third step was to choose the optimal strike price for the options. In mid-June, when this trade began to take shape, shares of Microsoft were trading in the $33–$35 range. I remember that I really wanted to have some downside protection for my obligation, so I was aiming for the $32 strike price instead of the $33 or the $34 ones. I waited patiently for a

drop in the price, and that drop arrived on June 24. I remember taking advantage of this decline and selling put options at the $32 strike price with the stock hovering slightly over $33. This meant that from the very beginning of the trade, the odds were in my favor, because the option was more than $1 out of the money ($33-and-some minus $32).

4) The fourth step was relatively easy—pick a time frame for the options. My rule of thumb is to stick with three-month time frames except in special circumstances. Nothing warranted a special deviation from my rule in this case—so I simply picked the option series that expired in September 2013. I wrote down the complete ID of the option that I picked and prepared the order that I would give to my broker in case I decided to execute the trade. The order would be to "**Sell to open the September 2013 put options on MSFT at the $32 strike price.**"

5) My fifth step was to calculate the potential return on this trade. I checked the price quote for the September $32 put option on Microsoft, and the quote on the screen showed $1.80. This meant that option sellers would get paid $1.80 to sell an option for a single share of Microsoft. But since option contracts only trade at multiples of a hundred, the more practical way to look at this would be that option sellers would get paid $180 to sell an

option that guarantees a purchase of $3,200 worth of Microsoft stock. All I did was multiply both the strike price ($32) and the cost ($1.80) by a hundred. Everything else remained equal.

I now put the numbers together. If I received a payment of $180 for a future (potential) obligation of $3,200, then my gross return on the trade would be 5.6 percent (180 divided by 3,200, times a hundred). This trade would last from June to September 2013, a total of three months.

This translates into an annualized return of a whopping 22.5 percent on my trade (5.6 percent times four). For me, such a return is more than satisfactory. I believe the same holds true for you as well.

6) The sixth step was to have a risk-and-reward plan before executing the trade. Just to refresh your memory, I was just bout to sell put options on Microsoft, at the $32 strike price, that expire on September 2013. We will be paid an up-front payment of $180 for each option contract we sell. This payment will obligate us to buy shares of Microsoft in the open market on September 2013, should their price drop below the predetermined $32.

How Our Trade Plays Out

There are three different scenarios that can play out on expiration day in September 2013:

1. **Share price of Microsoft is greater than $32**: We get to pocket the premium and have no obligation.

2. **Share price of Microsoft equals $32:** We get to pocket the premium and have no obligation.

3. **Share price of Microsoft is less than $32:** We get to pocket the premium, but we will also be obligated to buy shares at the predetermined price of $32. Our effective buying price per share will end up being $30.20 ($32 minus $1.80). Since this is an excellent price to pay for the shares, we should be fine with that obligation.

These are the only possible three scenarios out there. And we're fine with any of them.

7) My seventh and final step was to check whether the sale of options on Microsoft corresponded with conventional rules of proper diversification. When I decided to sell options on Microsoft, I had three other open trade positions—the first was McDonald's (restaurants), the second was Wells Fargo (banking), and third was Medtronic (health care). In other words, I gained exposure to four different business segments that have little correlation between them.

I went through my seven-step strategy, and everything checked out OK. I gave an order to my broker to sell twenty options on Microsoft by using the following order: **"Sell to open twenty of the September 2013 put options on MSFT at the \$32 strike price."** I instantly received a handsome premium of \$3,600 (twenty times \$180) right into my trading account.

So what do you think happened on expiration day in September?

Shares of Microsoft hovered above \$32 on expiration day of September 2013. This means that scenario number one kicked in, and I wasn't obligated to go out and buy the shares. Remember that this outcome is no surprise. More than 85 percent of the trades we make will end up playing scenario number one. When you write clever insurance policies you aren't forced to pay up very often.

The trade on Microsoft that I've discussed in this chapter was successfully implemented by using my seven-step trading strategy. There's absolutely no reason why you shouldn't take advantage of my strategy and begin earning a monthly income for yourself.

Chapter 11: Options and Trading Psychology

In this chapter, we'll discuss how the psychology of the masses supports my strategy. You can make a great living selling options without knowing a thing about market psychology. But in my opinion, understanding the underlying forces of the markets makes you a better options seller. That's why it's worthwhile to devote a whole chapter to market psychology.

There's no greater force in the markets than the force of psychology. I truly believe that the collective minds of the crowds are, in fact, responsible for the majority of market failures that we often witness.

Our strategy, on the other hand, doesn't join the crowd mentality. It takes advantage of it. By doing so, it ensures that we will only take well-calculated risks at all times. In fact, in turmoil markets we will sell an even greater number of put options than we normally sell in a calm market. Market psychology underlines and supports my strategy in the following four aspects.

Aspect #1: People Are Irrational Gamblers

The only reason we can sell put options in the market is that there's sufficient demand for them. Traders who wish to witness a quick and robust move in the price of their options always like to gamble and buy options. You see, buying options—in contrast to selling options—is a money-losing proposition. And that's because the trader who buys an option must be right on three different aspects to make money.

First, he must be right on the direction of the underlying stock. If the trader buys a call option and the stock drops in price, his options will lose value, and he will lose money. So getting the direction right is obviously a must.

Second, our trader must be right not only on the direction of the movement but also on the extent of this movement.

If he bought a call option on Coke at a strike of $48 when shares were changing hands at $40, then shares of Coke must leap by 20 percent for our poor trader to make any money. From my experience with options, trying to guess the extent of stock movements always ends in disappointment.

Third, our trader must operate under vigorous time constraints. As you recall, one of the basic traits of an option is its limited life span. Every option has an expiration date. So let's assume that the trader who bought options on Coke did guess the movement correctly, and he also predicted the extent of the movement. But guess what? Shares of Coke did actually jump by 20 percent, but this leap happened in December. Unfortunately for our poor trader, he bought the November call options. Therefore, he loses every cent he put into this trade.

Now, please take a minute and think about that. For a trader to actually make money by buying options, the guy has to be an absolute magician. He must predict the direction of the movement (up or down) correctly. Then, he must also predict the extent of the movement. And finally, all the above must occur within a given time frame. If he misses by even a week, he makes no profit. In other words, the odds are extremely unfavorable to traders who buy options. All the stars must properly align in their favor before they actually see a dime of profit.

And that's precisely why option *selling* makes so much sense. It's the exact flip side of the coin. When you sell options, the odds are stacked on your side and not against you.

Aspect #2: The Crowd Effect

Sheep move in herds, and so do investors. When panic starts to spread, everyone begins to sell shares without giving too much thought to why they're really selling. This phenomenon of panic selling creates an interesting disparity in the markets. The disparity is that markets always drop much faster and harder than they rise. In other words, stock prices tend to rise slowly over time, but when panic hits, Mr. Market loses his head and can easily erase years of returns in a few quick weeks. We all have experienced this disparity many times over in our own personal portfolios.

So how does the crowd effect help us as options sellers?

That's a great question. The crowd effect helps us in two different ways.

One, fierce declines in the markets create panic, and panic increases the volatility of individual stocks. (If you don't remember what volatility means, take another look at chapter 2.) When volatility rises, so do the premiums on stock options. In simple words, volatility increases the price of all options. And that's how we get paid more for the same product (option) we sell. A time of panic is a great time to be an option seller.

Two, the crowd effect tends to push prices of stocks downhill very fast. We like market declines because they allow us to commit to a lower strike price. This greatly improves the odds that we will never actually have to buy the stock on expiration day. Think about this for a moment. Say you're an insurance company and the house you recently insured just got burnt in a terrible fire. Would you rather the house were insured for $200,000 or for only $150,000? The answer is obvious. As an insurance company you want to be on the hook for as little as possible.

If we apply this example to the stock market, the question remains pretty much the same. Would you rather commit to purchase shares of Microsoft at the $32 strike or at the $28 strike? The answer is obvious here also—the lower the price, the better. And that's exactly why market declines do us only good. They allow us to collect a higher premium *and* to make a much more lenient commitment. This is the best of both worlds.

Aspect #3: Perception of Risk

Many studies have been conducted on the subject of how people perceive risk. One of the most interesting findings is that people consistently attribute a higher degree of risk to a single, large, one-time event than to smaller events that might occur more frequently and consistently.

By following these lines of reasoning, people also believe that a plane crash is more likely than a car accident.

But that's simply not true. The underlying concept that causes people to make this mistaken judgment is the irrationally high fear associated with large, scary events. On the way, they always tend to ignore the real risks awaiting them.

This erroneous perception of risk also dominates the financial markets. Investors and traders are always scared of single, large losses that might wipe out their trading accounts. In the meantime, they're very comfortable with risking small amounts of money and consistently losing it by betting when the odds are stacked against them.

And that's precisely why my strategy will continue to be profitable. We sell options to people who desire to risk little capital with the hope that they can beat the odds. In most cases, they don't. They lose the money they put on the trade, and then they go on and make another silly bet. They justify it by telling themselves that they've risked only little money, not the big money. What happens eventually is that they get poorer slowly instead of getting rich fast.

Aspect #4: Instant Gratification

The majority of traders believe that the market is there to satisfy their needs and desires. They believe that the market is some sort of a money machine that cares about their entry and exit points and that it basically exists to make them money. Because of this belief, they always yearn for some quick moves in stock prices. To make their potential profits even greater, they bet on these moves via the options market.

There's nothing like the feeling of exuberance that overcomes them when their option doubles in price practically overnight. It satisfies their need for instant gratification. But the trouble is that the market isn't there to take care of them. So for every time one of their options doubles in price, they've ten other options that lose 100 percent of their value. They will keep betting, only to go back to break-even point, which always seems to elude them. They are basically trapped in a vicious cycle of instant gratification and embarrassing losses.

By selling options and taking the opposite side of this trade, we position ourselves to make consistent money. Put simply, we take great advantage of the urgent need for instant gratification that the crowd of traders has.

In conclusion, fear, greed, and impatience are the three most harmful, yet common traits of traders out there. My strategy takes advantage of these three traits, one by one. The first aspect above deals with the greed of option buyers; the second and third aspects deal with fears and misconceptions of the investing herd. Finally, the fourth aspect outlined above describes our advantage over impatient, yearning-for-action traders.

Chapter 12:
Four Very Important Don'ts

It has been my experience that the things I should *not* do matter more than things I should do. As long as you follow the basic rules of my strategy you can become a really profitable trader or a less profitable trader, but you will make money either way. In contrast, if you break the rules of what you should *not* do, you simply won't survive financially. You will wipe out your account and some more.

The purpose of this chapter is to go into great detail on practices that you should not pursue. This chapter is extremely helpful to novice traders, but experienced traders can greatly benefit from it too. So please pay close attention to what I'm about to discuss with you in this chapter.

Don't #1: Do Not Trade with Your Rent Money

You should never trade with money that you need for your ongoing expenses, what I call "rent money." This rule applies to any trading or investing whatsoever. There's a strong psychological rationale behind this rule. Rent money is scared money, and scared money never wins. In other words, if you put your rent money into a trade, you will end up getting scared and making mistakes because you're afraid to lose this money.

We aspire for the exact opposite mentality when we trade. We are always peaceful and at ease. We know that we have written clever insurance policies and sold them to silly gamblers. The odds are heavily stacked in our favor, and the time is our friend because it diminishes the price of the options we sold. We are patient and confident. You see, there's simply no way you can be patient and confident if you trade your rent money. So don't do it.

The truth is that my strategy is very light on capital outlay. You don't have to invest a lot of money up front, and that's why it's different from many other strategies that you might have learned in the past. But still, rent money is rent money. If you're short on cash for your groceries, wait until you accumulate sufficient funds, and then go out and implement my strategy. I promise it will only do you good.

Don't #2: Do Not Overleverage Your Trade

By now, you understand that options involve leverage. In fact, an option contract controls one hundred shares. This means that the total capital outlay is indeed relatively low, but the volatility is high. This is why you should never sell more options than you can afford to buy if your obligation becomes due.

In the example we used in chapter 5, we sold options on Intel shares. We received a premium of $93 in return for the obligation to purchase $2,300 worth of Intel shares in December should the price drop below $23. Up to now, I haven't told you anything new.

Now comes the big mistake that novice traders make all the time. They get tempted by the large up-front pay-out, and they guarantee more than they can afford. If we use the example above, you can sell a single option, receive $93 in return, and commit to a possible purchase of $2,300 worth of Intel shares. But what if, instead, you really want to be paid $1,860 and not just $93?

You are tempted by the high up-front payout, so you sell twenty options instead of one. Your transaction will probably go unnoticed because you don't have to put down that money now. You might have to put it down in three months. Suppose that three months have passed and for some idle reason shares of Intel are $22.50 on expiration day. Guess what? You have to come up with $46,000 (twenty times $2,300) to buy shares. Since you don't have that money available, you embarrass yourself and your broker. You end up a loser. Remember, you must always adjust the number of options you sell to the number of shares you might end up buying.

It's a common mistake that novice traders make. Since I want you to be consistently profitable, I want to warn you ahead of time of such mistakes. This is one of those big mistakes. No one's going to do business with you any more after that.

Don't #3: Do Not Be Stressful

This specific "don't" might seem to you like it doesn't belong on the list. But it's probably the most important item on this list. Once you sell options on a stock, anything can happen. This is the proper mind-set you should have while trading. Prices of stocks can go up, down, or stay the same, but nothing's going to happen to you. You've calculated your risk-reward ratio prior to entering the trade, and that's why every outcome is just fine with you.

The main problem with stress and anxiety (aside from high blood pressure) is that they cause you to make silly mistakes. Anxiety always tends to exacerbate things. Sometimes we sell a put option, and a couple of days later the price of the underlying shares drops below our obligation threshold. This might scare us off a bit and ignite a "sorrow and regret" cycle.

You have to learn to control your emotions. Always remember that every bet we take is a well-calculated bet and that it will eventually be awfully profitable. Since price swings do happen, you simply need to learn how to not do anything. That's right. The best response on your part toward market reactions and price swings is simply nothing. Chances are that between now and the time your obligation is due things will revert back to their old selves.

In other words—relax and stop taking the market so seriously. We have a plan B for everything.

Don't #4: Do Not Be Greedy

This "don't" is especially important. Remember that you learned how to choose the optimal strike price for the options you sell?

Well, guess what? Many traders don't take that piece of advice very seriously. What they do instead is they look at the table of premiums (option prices) and choose to sell options at the strike price that offers them the highest premium. Say, for example, that shares of Microsoft are trading at $32. Instead of selling options at the $32 area, they decide to go out and sell options at the $38 level. In reward for this, they receive a much higher up-front premium, which makes them very happy about what they just did.

The trouble only arises three months later when their obligation comes to hunt them down. With such a large gap between current market price ($32) and the strike price of the option they sold ($38), it's a sure thing that they will be obligated to buy in their shares and wait a great deal of time before they're at break-even point. Selling deep-in-the-money options is a dangerous practice. That's an abuse of my strategy.

Never be greedy, and always sell options at the strike price at or around the prevailing market price of the shares. Don't be tempted to sell in-the-money options just for the fat premium. It's pure greed.

Chapter 13:
Trading and You

If you're like most folks out there, I'm sure that at some point you have tried to "swing for the fences"—aiming for a quick 50 percent on your trades using all types of susceptible strategies. I know I have. But once I mastered the skill of option selling and created my seven-step strategy, I stopped doing that.

Remember, my strategy isn't about home runs—it's about beating 95 percent of the traders out there while earning a nice monthly income for myself.

I can now easily beat the market, 2 percent at a time. And so can you.

If you take the time, read my book over, and learn my techniques carefully, there's no reason why you shouldn't make annual safe and steady double-digit returns like I have.

I want to quickly go over what you have learned in this book and how you can put it into good use, effective immediately.

I began my book by explaining why your broker and financial advisor would never tell you about my option-selling strategy. I have taught you the essential basics of the language of options. I then thoroughly elaborated on why selling options makes so much sense and why it's preferable to other trading strategies.

I then explained the cornerstones of my strategy—acting as the insurance company and as the house in a casino filled with gamblers. Once you grasped the idea of running an insurance company, I explained in detail my seven-step strategy, which consistently beats the market. I then taught you what do when things go wrong (as they do sometimes), and how to turn a losing trade into a winner.

The next stage was to guide you hand in hand on the specific instructions that you should give your broker when you execute my strategy. You learned how to place a trade and how to close it. You even read a useful chapter of technical analysis and how it can support your decision-making process.

You then read about a real trade that I placed—from start to finish, going through all the seven steps in my strategy. You followed one step at a time and saw how my strategy is translated into a real trade in the markets. The next stage was for you to learn about trading psychology. I hope that I was successful in convincing you that my strategy has deep roots in the psychology of human nature. It takes advantage of very aggressive human traits like fear, greed, and the desire for instant gratification. What's even more important in that chapter is that you learned that my strategy is likely to continue making money for you and me, regardless of the number of people who read this book and are "on to the secret" (hint: it's human nature to gamble).

And finally, the most important chapter describes in detail what you should *not* do with my strategy. Those four don'ts should keep you away from harm's way and on the highway to success. Remember, there are some very successful trading strategies out there that have been abused by novice traders, who later blamed the strategies for their lack of success. I don't want that to happen to you. Stick with the rules and prosper.

Having said that, the ball is now in your court—and it's your turn to play. Remember, this isn't some theoretical book about the markets. If you wanted to buy a book by an academic you probably wouldn't have picked up this book in the first place. This is a very practical guide on how to make a living by selling options.

If you wish to reach out for me with any question you might have, please don't hesitate. I'm always here for you at – *Sellingoptionsforaliving@gmail.com*

Trade well,

Shmulik Karpf

Appendix

Several times in the book, I referred to my favorite-stock list. I personally advise using this list before selling equity options. I always try to sell options on candidates on this list, and only very rarely will I sell options on stocks that are outside the list.

In order to make it into this list, a company must meet various rigid conditions. First, it must have a market cap of at least $50 billion. Such a massive market cap ensures that the company has been around for long enough and that it's selling something the world needs. Such a large scale is usually a sign of stability. Second, it must pay hefty dividends. I like to see a dividend yield of at least two times the average dividend yield of the S&P 500. Third, and most importantly, it must dominate its market. It has been my experience that stocks of companies that dominate their markets suffer only little when others might suffer a lot. These are the ultimate candidates on which we like to write insurance policies.

Below is my personal list of companies and their tickers. There's no significance to the order in which they are listed.

1. The Coca-Cola Company (KO)

2. Microsoft Corporation (MSFT)

3. Intel Corporation (INTC)

4. The Hershey Company (HSY)

5. Kraft Foods Group (KRFT)

6. International Business Machines (IBM)

7. ConocoPhillips (COP)

8. AbbVie (ABBV)

9. Apple (AAPL)

10. British Petroleum (BP)

11. Caterpillar (COP)

12. Chevron (CVX)

13. Cisco Systems (CSCO)

14. Eli Lilly (LLY)

15. Johnson and Johnson (JNJ)

16. Exxon Mobil (XOM)

17. McDonald's Corporation (MCD)

18. Novartis (NVS)

19. The Procter and Gamble Company (PG)

20. Wal-Mart Stores (WMT)

21. Wells Fargo (WFC)

22. Medtronic (MDT)

23. Abbott Laboratories (ABT)

24. CVS Caremark Corporation (CVS)

25. Exelon Corporation (EXC)

My list of twenty-five stocks is comprised of companies from a large variety of industries—from banking to restaurants. This gives me the flexibility to choose the right sector for me to insure at the right time. And again, this isn't a closed list. From time to time I may update the list and add or remove stocks to it and from it.

About the Author

Shmulik Karpf is a renowned trader and securities analyst based in Israel. He worked as a Securities analyst at the Tel Aviv Stock Exchange, and is currently serving as an equity analyst at Leumi Global Markets. For several years now, Shmulik has been a well read and closely followed contributor on leading financial sites like *Seeking Alpha* and *Investing.com*. He holds a B.A in Economics and Law, and an L.L.M in Commercial Litigation - both from the Hebrew University of Jerusalem.

www.ingramcontent.com/pod-product-compliance
Lightning Source LLC
Chambersburg PA
CBHW051328170526
45166CB00002B/729